AIRFRYER DINNER RECIPES

By Sarah Flores

The trademarks that are used are without any consent, and the publication of the trademark is without permission or backing by the trademark owner. All trademarks and brands within this book are for clarifying purposes only and are the owned by the owners themselves, not affiliated with this document.

Disclaimer and Terms of Use: The Author and Publisher has strived to be as accurate and complete as possible in the creation of this book, notwithstanding the fact that he does not warrant or represent at any time that the contents within are accurate due to the rapidly changing nature of the Internet. While all attempts have been made to verify information provided in this publication, the Author and Publisher assumes no responsibility for errors, omissions, or contrary interpretation of the subject matter herein.

Any perceived slights of specific persons, peoples, or organizations are unintentional. In practical advice books, like anything else in life, there are no guarantees of results. Readers are cautioned to rely on their own judgment about their individual circumstances and act accordingly.

This book is not intended for use as a source of legal, medical, business, accounting or financial advice. All readers are advised to seek services of competent professionals in the legal, medical, business, accounting, and finance fields.

TABLE OF CONTENTS

1. HEALTHY RECIPES

VEGETABLE TOTS

Serves: 4

Cook Time: 10 minutes

INGREDIENTS:

- 1 zucchini, peeled
- 1 carrot, peeled
- 1 large egg
- ¼ cup breadcrumbs
- ¼ cup Parmesan cheese, low sodium
- ¼ tsp. black pepper

DIRECTIONS::

1. Preheat air fryer to 400° F.
2. Grate zucchini and carrot. Wring out the excess water.
3. In a medium bowl, combine all the above Ingredients.
4. Form tots and place in air fryer as one layer.
5. Bake for 10 minutes.

HAM & EGG TOAST CUPS

Serves: 4

Cook Time: 15 minutes

INGREDIENTS:

- 1 zucchini, peeled
- 1 carrot, peeled
- 1 large egg
- ¼ cup breadcrumbs
- ¼ cup Parmesan cheese, low sodium
- ¼ tsp. black pepper

DIRECTIONS::

1. Firstly, brush the interior of the ramekin with a generous amount of butter with a cooking brush. Seriously. The more butter, the easier it is to remove the toast cups from the ramekins.

2. Flatten 8 slices of toast with either a rolling pin or your own palm. Make it as flat as possible

3. Line the inside of each ramekin with a slice of flattened toast.

4. Place another slice of flattened toast on top of the first toast and likewise, try to flatten the extra folds.

5. Cut 2 slices of ham into 8 smaller strips.

6. Line 2 strips of ham in each ramekin.

7. Crack an egg into each toast cup

8. Add a pinch of salt and some ground black pepper into each egg

9. You may also add some cheese into the toast cup

10. Place all 4 ramekins into the Airfryer for 15 mins at 160 degrees. You do not need to preheat the Airfryer in advance

11. Once done, remove the ramekins from the Airfryer with either a tea towel, silicone tongs or whatever kitchen contraception you have that protects your fingers from the heat.

12. To remove the toast cup from the ramekins, you can use a small knife and slowly sliced it round the inside of the ramekin just in case some bread got stuck to the sides. Then wriggled the toast cup out of the ramekin with the same small knife and a spoon.

SPANISH FRITTATA

Serves: 4

Cook Time: 20 minutes

INGREDIENTS:

- 3 jumbo free-range eggs
- ½ chorizo sausage – sliced
- 1 big potato – par-boiled and cubed
- ½ cup frozen corn
- olive oil
- chopped herbs of your choice – I used parsley
- ½ wheel of feta
- salt/pepper

DIRECTIONS:

1. Pour a good glug of olive oil in the pan of the Air Fryer(or your pan on the stove), and add the chorizo, corn and the potato. Set the Air Fryer on 180C and cook the sausage and potato until slightly browned. Break the 3 eggs into a little bowl and beat with a fork.

2. Season with salt and pepper. Pour eggs over the potato and sausage in the pan and top with crumbed feta and chopped parsley. Cook for another 5 minutes, check and if needed cook for another minute or so.

3. When cooked turn out on a plate and serve with a chunky tomato relish and some fresh rocket.

4. If you are doing it on the stove top and oven, preheat the oven to 180C and then cook the potato and sausage in a oven-proof pan on the stove top. When the potato has browned slightly, beat the eggs in a small bowl and pour over the potato and sausage.

5. Top with feta and parsley and and bake in the oven until the eggs are set.

AIR FRYER
POTATOES

Serves: 4

Cook Time: 5 minutes

INGREDIENTS:

- 2 medium sized Russet potatoes (~13 ounces total or roughly 2 generous cups), chopped in roughly one inch pieces

- A few generous spritzes of oil spray

- Pinch salt & pepper

- 1 small bell pepper (~5 ounces or roughly ¾ cup), chopped medium

- 1 small onion (~4 ounces or roughly ¾ cup), chopped medium

DIRECTIONS:

1. Put potatoes into air fryer basket. Spritz with oil spray, shake, spritz again, and add a pinch of salt.

2. Set the air fryer to 400 degrees and ten minutes. Stop once to shake during cooking time. (Feel free to stir, if the potatoes aren)t moving around enough.)

3. After the potatoes have cooked for ten minutes, add the bell pepper and onions. Add another spritz of oil, and shake basket. Set the air fryer to 400 degrees and 15 minutes.

4. During the last 5 minutes of cooking, check on the potatoes to make sure they aren't getting too brown. Depending on the size of your potatoes, you may need slightly less or slightly more time. If needed, add a few more minutes to the cooking time.

5. Add salt to taste and serve.

HASH BROWNS

Serves: 4

Cook Time: 15 minutes

INGREDIENTS:

- Large potatoes - 4 - peeled and finely grated
- Corn flour - 2 tablespoon
- Salt - to taste
- Pepper powder - to taste
- Chili flakes - 2 teaspoon
- Garlic powder - 1 teaspoon (optional)
- Onion Powder - 1 teaspoon (optional)
- Vegetable Oil - 1 + 1 teaspoon

DIRECTIONS:

1. Soak the shredded potatoes in cold water. Drain the water. Repeat the step to drain excess starch from potatoes.

2. In a non-stick pan heat 1 teaspoon of vegetable oil and saute shredded potatoes till cooked slightly for 3-4 mins.

3. Cool it down and transfer the potatoes to a plate.

4. Add corn flour, salt, pepper, garlic and onion powder and chili flakes

and mix together roughly.

5. Spread over the plate and pat it firmly with your fingers.

6. Regrigerate it for 20 minutes

7. Preheat air fryer at 180C

8. Take out the now refrigerated potato and divide into equal pieces with a knife

9. Brush the wire basket of the air fryer with little oil

10. Place the hash brown pieces in the basket and fry for 15 minutes at 180C

11. Take out the basket and flip the hash browns at 6 minutes so that they are air fried uniformly

12. Serve it hot with ketchup

AIR FRYER
FRENCH TOAST STICKS

Serves: 4

Cook Time: 15 minutes

INGREDIENTS:

- 4 pieces of sliced bread - whatever kind and thickness desired

- 2 Tbsp approximately of soft butter or margarine for buttering bread

- 2 eggs gently beaten

- salt

- cinnamon

- nutmeg

- ground cloves

- icing sugar and/or maple syrup for garnish and serving

DIRECTIONS:

1. Preheat Airfryer to 180* Celsius

2. In a bowl, gently beat together two eggs, a sprinkle of salt, a few heavy shakes of cinnamon, and small pinches of both nutmeg and ground cloves

3. Butter both sides of bread slices and cut into strips

4. Dredge each strip in the egg mixture and arrange in Airfryer (you will have to cook in two batches)

5. After 2 minutes of cooking, pause the Airfryer, take out the pan, making sure you place the pan on a heat safe surface, and spray the bread with cooking spray

6. Once you have generously coated the strips, flip and spray the second side as well

7. Return pan to fryer and cook for 4 more minutes, checking after a couple minutes to ensure they are cooking evenly and not burning

8. When egg is cooked and bread is golden brown, remove from Airfryer and serve immediately.

9. To garnish and serve, sprinkle with icing sugar, top with whip cream, drizzle with maple syrup, or serve with a small bowl of syrup for dipping

AIR-FRIED
SHISHITO PEPPERS

Serves: 4

Cook Time: 15 minutes

INGREDIENTS:

- 1-6 oz bag shishito peppers

- salt and pepper to taste

- ½ tablespoon avocado oil

- ⅓ cups Asiago cheese, grated fine

- limes

DIRECTIONS:

1. Rinse peppers with water and pat dry with paper towel. Place in bowl and toss with avocado oil, salt, and pepper. Place in air fryer and cook at 350 for 10 minutes. Watch carefully. You want them to come out blistered looking but not burnt.

2. Place shishito peppers on serving platter. Drizzle with a little lime juice and top with grated asiago cheese. Serve!

AIR FRYER
SPICY CHICKEN EMPANADAS

Serves: 4

Cook Time: 15 minutes

INGREDIENTS:

- 1 box of Refrigerated Pie Crust (2 rolls)
- 1 cup of shredded rotisserie Chicken
- 1 /2cup of shredded Cheddar Cheese
- 1 /4cups of chopped Green Onion/Scallions
- 1 /2cup of chopped Cilantro
- 2 chopped Jalapeno, seeds and membrane removed
- 1 /2teaspoon of Garlic Powder
- 1 /2teaspoon of ground Cumin
- 2 teaspoons of Hot Sauce
- Salt and pepper to taste
- Egg wash (1 egg whisked with 1 Tablespoon water)
- 1 /2cup of Sour Cream
- 1 teaspoon of chopped Green Onion/Scallion
- 1 /2cup of chopped Cilantro

- 1 /4teaspoon of Cayenne Pepper

- 1 /4teaspoon of smoked Paprika

- Salt to taste

DIRECTIONS:

1. In a large bowl, combine shredded chicken, cheddar cheese, chopped green onions, jalapeno and cilantro, garlic powder, ground cumin, hot sauce and salt and pepper. Mix well.

2. Unroll the pie dough onto a well-floured surface. Using a 5-inch circular cookie cutter, cut out as many circles as possible. Using a rolling-pin, roll out the scraps and continue to cut out circles until the dough runs out. We got 10 circles from 1 pie dough. Repeat the same with the other pie dough.

3. Spoon about 1 tablespoon of the spicy chicken filling into middle of dough. Moisten edges with egg wash.

4. Fold the dough in half over the filling, forming a half circle, then use the fingers to gently press and seal the edges. Use a fork to crimp the edges together.

5. Brush each empanadas with the egg wash.

6. Air fry the empanadas at 400 F for 10 minutes.

7. Serve hot with Cilantro-Scallion Dipping Sauce.

COCONUT SHRIMP WITH SPICY MARMALADE SAUCE

Serves: 4

Cook Time: 20 minutes

INGREDIENTS:

- 8 large shrimp, shelled and deveined
- 8 ounces coconut milk
- ½ cup shredded, sweetened coconut
- ½ cup panko bread
- ½ teaspoon cayenner pepper
- ¼ teaspoon kosher salt
- ¼ teaspoon fresh ground pepper
- ½ cup orange marmalade
- 1 tablespoon honey
- 1 teaspoon mustard
- ¼ teaspoon hot sauce

DIRECTIONS:

1. Clean the shrimp and set aside.

2. In a small bowl, whisk the coconut milk and season with salt and pepper. Set aside. In a separate small bowl, whisk together the coconut, panko, cayenne pepper, salt and pepper.

3. One at a time, dip the shrimp in the coconut milk, the panko and then place in the basket of the fryer. Repeat until all the shrimp are coated. Cook the shrimp in the fryer for 20 minutes at 350 degrees or until the shrimp are cooked through.

4. While the shrimp are cooking, whisk together the marmalade, honey, mustard and hot sauce.

5. Serve the shrimp with the sauce immediately.

AIR FRYER 3 INGREDIENT FRIED CATFISH

Serves: 4

Cook Time: 60 minutes

INGREDIENTS:

- 4 catfish fillets
- ¼ cup seasoned fish fry
- 1 tbsp olive oil
- 1 tbsp chopped parsley optional

DIRECTIONS:

1. Preheat Air Fryer to 400 degrees.

2. Rinse the catfish and pat dry.

3. Pour the fish fry seasoning in a large Ziploc bag.

4. Add the catfish to the bag, one at a time. Seal the bag and shake. Ensure the entire filet is coated with seasoning.

5. Spray olive oil on the top of each filet.

6. Place the filet in the Air Fryer basket. (Due to the size of my fillets, I cooked each one at a time). Close and cook for 10 minutes.

7. Flip the fish. Cook for an additional 10 minutes.

8. Flip the fish.

9. Cook for an additional 2-3 minutes or until desired crispness.

10. Top with parsley.

JALAPEÑO POPPERS

Serves: 4

Cook Time: 20 minutes

INGREDIENTS:

- 10 jalapeno peppers, halved and deseeded
- 8 oz of cream cheese
- ¼ c fresh parsley
- ¾ c gluten-free tortilla or bread crumbs

DIRECTIONS:

1. Mix together ½ of crumbs and cream cheese. Once combined add in the parsley.

2. Stuff each pepper with this mixture.

3. Gently press the tops of the peppers into the remaining ¼ c of crumbs to create the top coating.

4. Cook in an air fryer at 370 degrees F for 6-8 minutes OR in a conventional oven at 375 degrees F for 20 minutes.

5. Let cool and ENJOY!

PORK TAQUITOS

Serves: 4

Cook Time: 20 minutes

INGREDIENTS:

- 30 oz. of cooked shredded pork tenderloin

- 2 ½ cups fat free shredded mozzerella

- 10 small flour tortillas

- 1 lime, juiced

- Cooking spray

- Salsa for dipping (optional)

- Sour Cream (optional)

- Simple Living Products Air Fryer

DIRECTIONS:

1. Preheat air fryer to 380 degrees.

2. Sprinkle lime juice over pork and gently mix around.

3. Microwave 5 tortillas at a time with a damp paper towel over it for 10 seconds, to soften.

4. Add 3 oz. of pork and ¼ cup of cheese to a tortilla.

5. Tightly and gently roll up the tortillas.

6. Line tortillas on a greased foil lined pan.

7. Spray an even coat of cooking spray over tortillas.

8. Air Fry for 7-10 minutes until tortillas are a golden color, flipping half way through.

9. 2 taquitos per serving WW SP - 8.

10. Weight Watchers Smart Points calculated using Weight Watchers recipe builder.

11. But in case you don›t have an air fryer, they can also be baked in the oven for 7 - 10 minutes on 375 degrees.

FISH FINGER SANDWICH

Serves: 4

Cook Time: 15 minutes

INGREDIENTS:

- 4 small cod fillets (skin removed)
- salt and pepper
- 2 tbsp flour
- 40g dried breadcrumbs
- spray oil
- 250g frozen peas
- 1 tbsp creme fraiche or greek yogurt
- 10-12 capers
- squeeze of lemon juice
- 4 bread rolls or 8 small slices of bread

DIRECTIONS:

1. Pre-heat the Optimum HealthyFry Air Fryer.

2. Take each of the cod fillets, season with salt and pepper and lightly dust in the flour. Then roll quickly in the breadcrumbs. The idea is to get a light coating of breadcrumbs on the fish rather than a thick layer.

Repeat with each cod fillet.

3. Add a few sprays of oil spray to the bottom of the fryer basket. Place the cod fillets on top and cook on the fish setting (200c) for 15 mins.

4. Whilst the fish is cooking, cook the peas in boiling water for a couple of minutes on the hob or in the microwave. Drain and then add to a blender with the creme fraiche, capers and lemon juice to taste. Blitz until combined.

5. Once the fish has cooked, remove it from the HealthyFry Air Fryer and start layering your sandwich with the bread, fish and pea puree. You can also add lettuce, tartar sauce and any other of your favourite toppings!

TACO BELL CRUNCH WRAPS

Serves: 4

Cook Time: 10 minutes

INGREDIENTS:

- 2 lbs ground beef
- 2 packets taco seasoning
- 1 ⅓ c water
- 6 12 inch flour tortillas
- 3 roma tomatoes
- 12 oz nacho cheese
- 2 c shredded lettuce
- 2 c Mexican blend cheese
- 2 c sour cream
- 6 to stadas
- Olive oil or butter spray

DIRECTIONS:

1. Preheat air fryer to 400°F
2. Prepare ground beef according to taco seasoning packet

3. In the center of each flour tortilla with 2/3 c of beef, 4 tbs of nacho cheese, 1 tostada, ⅓ c sour cream, ⅓ c of lettuce. 1/6th of the tomatoes and ⅓ c cheese

4. To close, flood the edges up, over the center, it should look sort of like a pinwheel

5. Repeat 2 and 3 with remaining wraps

6. Lay folded side down in your air fryer

7. Spray with oil

8. Cook for 2 mins or until brown

9. Using a spatula, carefully flip and spray again

10. Cook an additional 2 mins and repeat with remaining wraps

11. Allow to cool a few mins and enjoy.

SRIRACHA HONEY CHICKEN WINGS

Serves: 4

Cook Time: 35 minutes

INGREDIENTS:

- 1 pound chicken wings, tips removed and wings cut into individual drummettes and flats.

- ¼ cup honey

- 2 tablespoons sriracha sauce

- 1 ½ tablespoons soy sauce

- 1 tablespoon butter

- juice of ½ lime

- cilantro, chives, or scallions for garnish

DIRECTIONS:

1. Preheat the air fryer to 360 degrees F. Add the chicken wings to the air fryer basket, and cook for 30 minutes, turning the chicken about every 7 minutes with tongs to make sure the wings are evenly browned.

2. While the wings are cooking, add the sauce Ingredients to a small sauce pan and bring to a boil for about 3 minutes.

3. When the wings are cooked, toss them in a bowl with the sauce until fully coated, sprinkle with the garnish, and serve immediately.

2. MEATS

AIR FRIED TURKEY BREAST WITH CHERRY GLAZE

Serves: 4

Cook Time: 25 minutes

INGREDIENTS:

- 1 (5-pound) turkey breast
- 2 teaspoons olive oil
- 1 teaspoon dried thyme
- ½ teaspoon dried sage
- 1 teaspoon salt
- ½ teaspoon freshly ground black pepper
- ½ cup cherry preserves
- 1 tablespoon chopped fresh thyme leaves
- 1 teaspoon soy sauce
- freshly ground black pepper

DIRECTIONS:

1. You'll need a larger air fryer (5-quart air fryer or bigger) to make this recipe. If you have a 3-quart air fryer, you can cook a 3-pound bone-in split turkey breast.

2. Just cut the seasonings and glaze Ingredients in half, and you may need to trim a little of the base of the breast bone away so that it fits into your air fryer basket.

3. Don't worry if it's a tight fit because the turkey will shrink a little once it is cooked, so it will be easier to turn when the time comes.

4. Cook for 20 minutes breast side up, then 20 minutes breast side down and finally another 15 minutes breast side up. Then, glaze the turkey and cook it for 5 more minutes.

TURKEY BREAST WITH MAPLE MUSTARD GLAZE

Serves: 4

Cook Time: 30 minutes

INGREDIENTS:

- 2 teaspoons olive oil
- 5-pound whole turkey breast
- 1 teaspoon dried thyme
- ½ teaspoon dried sage
- ½ teaspoon smoked paprika
- 1 teaspoon salt
- ½ teaspoon freshly ground black pepper
- ¼ cup maple syrup
- 2 tablespoon Dijon mustard
- 1 tablespoon butter

DIRECTIONS:

1. Pre heat air fryer to 350°F.
2. Brush the olive oil all over the turkey breast.
3. Combine the thyme, sage, paprika, salt and pepper and rub the outside of the turkey breast with the spice mixture.

4. Transfer the seasoned turkey breast to the air fryer basket and air-fry at 350°F for 25 minutes. Turn the turkey breast on its side and air-fry for another 12 minutes. Turn the turkey breast on the opposite side and air-fry for another 12 minutes. The internal temperature of the turkey breast should reach 165°F when fully cooked.

5. While the turkey is air-frying, combine the maple syrup, mustard and butter in a small saucepan. When the cooking time is up, return the turkey breast to an upright position and brush the glaze all over the turkey. Air-fry for a final 5 minutes, until the skin is nicely browned and crispy. Let the turkey rest, loosely tented with foil, for at least 5 minutes before slicing and serving.

CHICKEN CHEESESTEAK STROMBOLI

Serves: 4

Cook Time: 20 minutes

INGREDIENTS:

- ½ onion, sliced

- 1 teaspoon vegetable oil

- 2 boneless, skinless chicken breasts, partially frozen and sliced very thin on the bias (about 1 pound)

- 1 tablespoon Worcestershire sauce

- salt and freshly ground black pepper

- 14 ounces pizza dough (store-bought or homemade)

- 1½ cup grated Cheddar cheese

- ½ cup Cheese (or other jarred cheese sauce), warmed gently in the microwave

DIRECTIONS:

1. Pre-heat the air fryer to 400°F.

2. Toss the sliced onion with oil and air-fry for 8 minutes, stirring halfway through the cooking time. Add the sliced chicken and Worcestershire sauce to the air fryer basket, and toss to evenly distribute the Ingredients. Season the mixture with salt and freshly ground black

pepper and air-fry for 8 minutes, stirring a couple of times during the cooking process. Remove the chicken and onion from the air fryer and let the mixture cool a little.

3. On a lightly floured surface, roll or press the pizza dough out into a 13-inch by 11-inch rectangle, with the long side closest to you. Sprinkle half of the Cheddar cheese over the dough leaving an empty 1-inch border from the edge farthest away from you. Top the cheese with the chicken and onion mixture, spreading it out evenly. Drizzle the cheese sauce over the meat and sprinkle the remaining Cheddar cheese on top.

4. Start rolling the stromboli away from you and toward the empty border. Make sure the filling stays tightly tucked inside the roll. Finally, tuck the ends of the dough in and pinch the seam shut. Place the seam side down and shape the Stromboli into a U-shape to fit in the air fry basket. Cut 4 small slits with the tip of a sharp knife evenly in the top of the dough and lightly brush the stromboli with a little oil.

5. Pre-heat the air fryer to 370°F.

6. Spray or brush air fryer basket with oil and transfer the U-shaped stromboli to the air fryer basket. Air-fry for 12 minutes, turning the stromboli over halfway through the cooking time. (Use a plate to invert the stromboli out of the air fryer basket and then slide it back into the basket off the plate.)

7. To remove carefully flip stromboli over onto a cutting board. Let it rest for a couple of minutes before serving. Slice the stromboli into 3-inch pieces and serve with ketchup for dipping if desired.

CHEESEBURGERS

Serves: 4

Cook Time: 20 minutes

INGREDIENTS:

- 12 ounces (¾ pound) lean ground beef
- 3 tablespoons minced onion
- 4 teaspoons ketchup
- 2 teaspoons yellow mustard
- salt and freshly ground black pepper
- 4 slices of Cheddar cheese, broken into smaller pieces
- 8 hamburger dill pickle chips

DIRECTIONS:

1. Combine the ground beef, minced onion, ketchup, mustard, salt and pepper in a large bowl. Mix well to thoroughly combine the Ingredients. Divide the meat into four equal portions.

2. To make the stuffed burgers, flatten each portion of meat into a thin patty. Place 4 pickle chips and half of the cheese onto the center of two of the patties, leaving a rim around the edge of the patty exposed. Place the remaining two patties on top of the first and press the meat together firmly, sealing the edges tightly. With the burgers on a flat surface, press the sides of the burger with the palm of your hand to create a straight edge. This will help keep the stuffing inside the burger while it cooks.

3. Pre-heat the air fryer to 370°F.

4. Place the burgers inside air fryer basket and air-fry for 20 minutes, flipping the burgers over halfway through the cooking time.

5. Serve the cheeseburgers on buns with lettuce and tomato.

HAM WITH MUSTARD

Serves: 4

Cook Time: 25 minutes

INGREDIENTS:

- 1 joint of ham, approximately 750 g
- 2 tablespoons honey
- 2 tablespoons French mustard
- 200 ml whiskey

DIRECTIONS:

1. Remove the ham from the refrigerator half an hour before cooking to bring to room temperature. Take a casserole dish that fits in the Airfryer and make the marinade. For the marinade, mix the whiskey, honey and mustard.

2. Place the ham in the oven dish and turn it in the marinade. Heat the Airfryer to 160 degrees and cook the ham for 15 minutes.

3. Add another shot of whiskey and turn in the marinade again. Cook the ham for 25 minutes until done at 160 degrees.

4. Great with potatoes and fresh vegetables from the Airfryer.

SPICY
ROLLED MEAT

Serves: 4

Cook Time: 40 minutes

INGREDIENTS:

- 1 pork fricandeau or turkey breast fillet - 500 g
- 1 clove garlic, crushed
- ½ teaspoon chili powder
- 1 teaspoon cinnamon
- 1½ teaspoon ground cumin
- 2 tablespoons olive oil
- 1 small red onion, finely chopped
- 3 tablespoons flat-leafed parsley, finely chopped
- String for rolled meat

DIRECTIONS:

1. Place the meat on a cutting board with the short side towards you and slit it horizontally along the full length about a ⅓ of the way from the top stopping 2 cm from the edge. Fold this part open and slit it again from this side and open it. You now have a long piece of meat.

2. Mix the garlic in a bowl with the chili powder, cinnamon, cumin, pepper and 1 teaspoon salt. Add the olive oil. Spoon 1 tablespoon of this mixture in another small bowl. Mix the onion and parsley in the mixture in the big bowl.

3. Preheat the airfryer to 180°C.

4. Coat the meat with the onion mixture. Roll the meat firmly, start at the short side. Tie the string around the meat at 3 cm intervals. Rub the outside of the rolled meat with the herb mixture.

VEAL ROLLS WITH SAGE

Serves: 4

Cook Time: 20 minutes

INGREDIENTS:

- 400 ml meat stock
- 200 ml dry white wine
- 4 veal cutlets
- Freshly ground pepper
- 8 fresh sage leaves
- 4 slices cured ham
- 25 g butter

DIRECTIONS:

1. Preheat the airfryer to 200°C. Boil the meat stock and the wine in a wide pan on medium heat until it has reduced to one-third of the original amount.

2. Sprinkle salt and pepper on the cutlets and cover them with the sage leaves. Firmly roll the cutlets and wrap a slice of ham around each cutlet.

3. Thinly brush the entire cutlets with butter and place them in the basket. Slide the basket into the airfryer and set the timer to 10 minutes. Roast the veal rolls until nicely brown.

4. Lower the temperature to 150°C and set the timer to 5 minutes. Roast the rolls until done. Mix the remainder of the butter with the reduced stock and season the gravy with salt and pepper.

5. Thinly slice the veal rolls and serve them with the gravy. Tasty with tagliatelle and green beans.

LAMB WITH MACADAMIA CRUST

Serves: 4

Cook Time: 30 minutes

INGREDIENTS:

- 1 garlic clove

- 1 tbsp olive oil

- 800 g rack of lamb

- pepper & salt

- 75 g unsalted macadamia nuts

- 1 tbsp breadcrumbs (preferably homemade)

- 1 tbsp chopped fresh rosemary

- 1 egg

DIRECTIONS:

1. Finely chop the garlic. Mix the olive oil and garlic to make garlic oil. Brush the rack of lamb with the oil and season with pepper & salt.

2. Preheat the Airfryer to 100°C.

3. Finely chop the nuts and place them into a bowl. Stir in the breadcrumbs and rosemary. Whisk the egg in another bowl.

4. To coat the lamb, dip the meat into the egg mixture, draining off any excess. Coat the lamb with the macadamia crust.

5. Put the coated lamb rack in the Airfryer basket and slide the basket into the Airfryer. Set the timer for 25 minutes. After 25 minutes, increase the temperature to 200°C and set the timer for another 5 minutes. Remove the meat and leave to rest, covered with aluminium foil, for 10 minutes before serving.

PORK TENDERLOIN WITH BELL PEPPER

Serves: 4

Cook Time: 20 minutes

INGREDIENTS:

- 1 red or yellow bell pepper, in thin strips
- 1 red onion, in thin slices
- 1 pork tenderloin - 300 g
- 2 teaspoons Provençal herbs
- Freshly ground black pepper
- 1 tablespoon olive oil
- ½ tablespoon mustard
- Round 15 cm oven dish

DIRECTIONS:

1. Preheat the airfryer to 200°C.

2. In the dish, mix the bell pepper strips with the onion, the Provençal herbs, and some salt and pepper to taste. Add ½ tablespoon olive oil to the mixture.

3. Cut the pork tenderloin into four pieces and rub with salt, pepper and mustard. Thinly coat the pieces with olive oil and place them upright in the dish on top of the pepper mixture.

4. Place the bowl in the basket and slide the basket into the airfryer. Set the timer to 15 minutes and roast the meat and the vegetables.

5. Turn the meat and mix the peppers halfway through the preparation time. Delicious with mashed potatoes and a fresh salad.

DRUMSTICKS WITH BARBECUE MARINADE

Serves: 4

Cook Time: 20 minutes

INGREDIENTS:

- 1 clove garlic, crushed
- ½ tablespoon mustard
- 2 teaspoons brown sugar
- 1 teaspoon chili powder
- Freshly ground black pepper
- 1 tablespoon olive oil
- 4 drumsticks

DIRECTIONS:

1. Preheat the AirFryer to 200°C.

2. Mix the garlic with the mustard, brown sugar, chili powder, a pinch of salt and freshly ground pepper to taste. Mix with the oil.

3. Rub the drumsticks completely with the marinade and leave to marinate for 20 minutes.

4. Put the drumsticks in the basket and slide the basket into the AirFryer. Set the timer to 10 minutes. Roast the drumsticks until brown.

5. Then lower the temperature to 150°C and roast the drumsticks for another 10 minutes until done.

6. Serve the drumsticks with corn salad and French bread.

CHICKEN FILLET WITH CURED HAM AND BRIE

Serves: 4

Cook Time: 20 minutes

INGREDIENTS:

- 2 large chicken fillets

- Freshly ground pepper

- 4 small slices Brie cheese

- 1 tablespoon chives, finely chopped

- 4 slices cured ham

DIRECTIONS:

1. Preheat the airfryer to 180°C.

2. Cut the chicken fillets into four equal pieces and slit them horizontally to 1 cm from the edge. Open the chicken fillets and sprinkle with salt and pepper. Cover each piece with a slice of Brie and some chives.

3. Close the chicken fillets and tightly wrap a slice of ham around them. Thinly coat the stuffed fillets with olive oil and put them in the basket.

4. Slide the basket into the airfryer and set the timer to 15 minutes. Roast the chicken fillets nicely brown and done. Delicious with mashed potatoes and stir-fried witloof chicory.

MEAT LOAF

Serves: 4

Cook Time: 20 minutes

INGREDIENTS:

- 400 g (lean) ground beef
- 1 egg, lightly beaten
- 3 tablespoons bread crumbs
- 50 g salami or chorizo sausage, finely chopped
- 1 small onion, finely chopped
- 1 tablespoon (fresh) thyme
- Freshly ground pepper
- 2 mushrooms, thick slices

DIRECTIONS:

1. Preheat the AirFryer to 200°C.

2. Mix the ground meat in a bowl with the egg, bread crumbs, salami, onion, thyme, 1 teaspoon salt and a generous amount of pepper. Knead and mix thoroughly.

3. Transfer the ground meat to the pan or dish and smoothen the top. Press in the mushrooms and coat the top with olive oil.

4. Place the pan or dish in the basket and slide the basket into the AirFryer. Set the timer to 25 minutes and roast the meat loaf until nicely brown and done.

5. Leave the meat loaf to stand for at least 10 minutes before serving. Then cut the loaf into wedges. Tasty with fried potatoes and a salad.

LEG OF LAMB WITH POTATO QUENELLES AND BRUSSELS SPROUTS

Serves: 4

Cook Time: 120 minutes

INGREDIENTS:

- For the leg of lamb:
- 1 kg leg of lamb
- 2 spoons groundnut oil
- 15 g rosemary
- 15 g lemon thyme
- 1 garlic clove
- 600 g Brussels sprouts
- For the quenelles:
- 4 large potatoes
- A knob of butter
- Nutmeg

DIRECTIONS:

1. Take a nice leg of lamb, score and stud with a few large sprigs of rosemary and lemon thyme. Smear the leg with the groundnut oil. Heat the Airfryer to 150 degrees and cook the lamb for 75 minutes.

2. Potato quenelles are simple to make and, as I previously mentioned, can be prepared in advance and frozen. Mash the potatoes and season to taste adding milk, butter and nutmeg. Form the quenelles using two spoons, transferring the mash from one spoon to the other. If you choose to make the quenelles in advance, they need to cook for 15 minutes at 200 degrees. If you prepared them fresh, they only need 8 minutes.

3. Clean and tail the Brussels sprouts and mix with some honey and neutral oil. After 75 minutes cooking time, add the sprouts and the frozen quenelles to the Airfryer. Bake the lamb, sprouts and quenelles together for 15 minutes at 200 degrees. If you prepared the quenelles from fresh, just add them 7 minutes after the Brussels sprouts.

AIR FRYER SHRIMP

Serves: 4

Cook Time: 25 minutes

INGREDIENTS:

- 1 pound raw shrimp peeled and deveined
- 1 egg white 3 tbsp
- ½ cup all purpose flour
- ¾ cup panko bread crumbs
- 1 tsp paprika
- Chicken Seasoning to taste
- salt and pepper to taste
- cooking spray
- Bang Bang Sauce
- ⅓ cup plain, non-fat Greek yogurt
- 2 tbsp Sriracha
- ¼ cup sweet chili sauce

DIRECTIONS:

1. Preheat Air Fryer to 400 degrees.

2. Season the shrimp with the seasonings.

3. Place the flour, egg whites, and panko bread crumbs in three separate bowls.

4. Create a cooking stations. Dip the shrimp in the flour, then the egg whites, and the panko bread crumbs last.

5. When dipping the shrimp in the egg whites, you do not need to submerge the shrimp. Do a light dab so that most of the flour stays on the shrimp. You want the egg white to adhere to the panko crumbs.

6. Spray the shrimp with cooking spray. Do not spray directly on the shrimp. The panko will go flying. Keep a nice distance.

7. Add the shrimp to the Air Fryer basket. Cook for 4 minutes. Open the basket and flip the shrimp to the other side. Cook for an additional 4 minutes or until crisp.

HONEY & LIME CHICKEN STUFFED WITH ZUCCHINI

Serves: 4

Cook Time: 60 minutes

INGREDIENTS:

- 1 whole chicken

- For the filling:

- 2 tablespoons olive oil

- 2 red onions

- 1 green zucchini

- 1 yellow zucchini

- 1 sweet apple

- 2 apricots

- Fresh thyme

- For the marinade:

- 200 g honey

- Juice of 1 large lemon

- Freshly ground pepper

- Salt

DIRECTIONS:

1. Chop all the Ingredients for the filling into small cubes and mix with the oil in a bowl. Season to taste with salt and pepper. Fill the chicken with the mixture.

2. Heat the Airfryer to 200 degrees C. If you have the grill pan accessory you can use this to place the chicken on, so you have more space in your Airfryer. The Viva model fits a chicken of up to 1.2 kg; the Avance model up to 1.6 kg. Place the chicken in the Airfryer and sear the meat for 5 minutes.

3. Meanwhile, melt the honey in a pan with the juice of the lemon and season it to taste with salt and pepper. Take the chicken out of the Airfryer and cover it in some of the marinade. Set the temperature of the Airfryer to 150 degrees and put the chicken back in. Open the Airfryer every 15 minutes to cover the chicken with marinade until it has all gone.

4. After 60 minutes, the chicken will be cooked. There are two ways to check whether the chicken is cooked. Either with a meat thermometer (temperature must be 85 degrees) or by checking the color of the liquid. When cooked, the liquid will run clear and show no pink.

3. FAST AND EASY

ORANGE TOFU

Serves: 4

Cook Time: 25 minutes

INGREDIENTS:

- 1 pound extra-firm tofu drained and pressed (or use super-firm tofu)
- 1 Tablespoon tamari
- 1 Tablespoon cornstarch (or arrowroot powder)
- For the sauce:
- 1 teaspoon orange zest
- ⅓ cup orange juice
- ½ cup water
- 2 teaspoons cornstarch (or arrowroot powder)
- ¼ teaspoon crushed red pepper flakes
- 1 teaspoon fresh ginger minced
- 1 teaspoon fresh garlic minced
- 1 Tablespoon pure maple syrup

DIRECTIONS:

1. Cut the tofu in cubes.

2. Place the tofu cubes in a quart-size plastic storage bag. Add the tamari and seal the bag. Shake the bag until all the tofu is coated with the tamari.

3. Add the tablespoon of cornstarch to the bag. Shake again until the tofu is coated. Set the tofu aside to marinate for at least 15 minutes.

4. Meanwhile add all the sauce Ingredients to a small bowl and mix with a spoon. Set aside.

5. Place the tofu in the air fryer in a single layer. You will probably need to do this in two batches.

6. Cook the tofu at 390 degrees for 10 minutes, shaking it after 5 minutes.

7. After youьre done cooking the batches of tofu, add it all to a skillet over medium-high heat. Give the sauce a stir and pour it over the tofu. Stir the tofu and sauce until the sauce has thickened and the tofu is heated through.

8. Serve immediately with rice and steamed vegetables, if desired.

PANKO BREADED CHICKEN PARMESAN WITH MARINARA SAUCE

Serves: 4

Cook Time: 25 minutes

INGREDIENTS:

- 16 oz skinless chicken breasts sliced in half to make 4 breasts
- 1 cup panko bread crumbs
- ½ cup parmesan cheese grated
- ½ cup mozarella cheese shredded
- 1/8 cup egg whites
- ¾ cup marinara sauce see below for link to the recipe for homemade
- 2 tsp Italian Seasoning
- salt and pepper to taste
- cooking spray

DIRECTIONS:

1. Preheat the Air Fryer to 460. Spray the basket with cooking spray.

2. Slice the chicken breasts in half horizontally to create 4 thinner chicken breasts. Place the chicken breasts on a hard surface and pound them to completely flatten.

3. Grate the parmesan cheese.

4. Combine the panko breadcrumbs, cheese, and seasonings in a bowl large enough to dip the chicken breasts. Stir to combine.

5. Place the egg whites in a bowl large enough to dip the chicken.

6. Dip the chicken in the egg whites and then the breadcrumbs mixture.

7. Place in the Air Fryer. Spray the top of the chicken with cooking spray.

8. Cook for 7 minutes. Top each of the breasts with marinara sauce and the shredded mozzarella. Cook for an additional 3 minutes or until cheese has melted.

SWEET AND SOUR PORK

Serves: 4

Cook Time: 15 minutes

INGREDIENTS:

- 1 serving slice of fresh pineapple, cut in cubes
- 1 medium size onion, sliced
- 1 medium size tomato, cut in cubes
- 1 tbsp minced garlic
- 2 tbsp oyster sauce
- 2 tbsp of tomato sauce
- 1 tbsp of worchestire sauce
- Sugar to taste
- Plain flour
- 1 egg

DIRECTIONS:

1. Heat up the Airfryer at 120 degrees for 5 mins

2. When ready, dip pork in egg and then coat with plain flour.

3. Dust off any excess flour on the pork before placing into the frying basket.

4. Set timer to 20 minutes.

5. When it's done, set the meat aside to prepare the sauce.

CAJUN
SALMON

Serves: 4

Cook Time: 25 minutes

INGREDIENTS:

- 1 piece fresh salmon fillet (about 200g)

- Cajun seasoning (just enough to coat)

- A light sprinkle of sugar (optional)

- Juice from a quarter of lemon, to serve

DIRECTIONS:

1. Preheat your airfryer to 180C. For the Philips airfryer, the orange light will go off to indicate that the temperature has been reached. For other brands, typically just preheat for 5 minutes.

2. Clean your salmon and pat dry. In a plate, sprinkle Cajun seasoning all over and ensure all sides are coated. You don't need too much. If you prefer a tad of sweetness, add a light sprinkling of sugar. NO seasoning time required.

3. For a salmon fillet about ¾ of an inch thick, airfry for 7 minutes, skin side up on the grill pan. Serve immediately with a squeeze of lemon.

BOURBON BACON BURGER

Serves: 4

Cook Time: 25 minutes

INGREDIENTS:

- 1 tablespoon bourbon
- 2 tablespoons brown sugar
- 3 strips maple bacon, cut in half
- ¾ pound ground beef (80% lean)
- 1 tablespoon minced onion
- 2 tablespoons BBQ sauce
- ½ teaspoon salt
- freshly ground black pepper
- 2 slices Colby Jack cheese (or Monterey Jack)
- 2 Kaiser rolls
- lettuce and tomato, for serving
- Zesty Burger Sauce:
- 2 tablespoons BBQ sauce
- 2 tablespoons mayonnaise
- ¼ teaspoon ground paprika
- freshly ground black pepper

DIRECTIONS:

1. Pre-heat the air fryer to 390°F and pour a little water into the bottom of the air fryer drawer. (This will help prevent the grease that drips into the bottom drawer from burning and smoking.)

2. Combine the bourbon and brown sugar in a small bowl. Place the bacon strips in the air fryer basket and brush with the brown sugar mixture. Air-fry at 390°F for 4 minutes. Flip the bacon over, brush with more brown sugar and air-fry at 390°F for an additional 4 minutes until crispy.

3. While the bacon is cooking, make the burger patties. Combine the ground beef, onion, BBQ sauce, salt and pepper in a large bowl. Mix together thoroughly with your hands and shape the meat into 2 patties.

4. Transfer the burger patties to the air fryer basket and air-fry the burgers at 370°F for 15 to 20 minutes, depending on how you like your burger cooked (15 minutes for rare to medium-rare; 20 minutes for well-done). Flip the burgers over halfway through the cooking process.

5. While the burgers are air-frying, make the burger sauce by combining the BBQ sauce, mayonnaise, paprika and freshly ground black pepper to taste in a bowl.

6. When the burgers are cooked to your liking, top each patty with a slice of Colby Jack cheese and air-fry for an additional minute, just to melt the cheese. (You might want to pin the cheese slice to the burger with a toothpick to prevent it from blowing off in your air fryer.) Spread the sauce on the inside of the Kaiser rolls, place the burgers on the rolls, top with the bourbon bacon, lettuce and tomato and enjoy!

AIR FRYER
POTATO LATKES BITES

Serves: 4

Cook Time: 15 minutes

INGREDIENTS:

- 4 large Potatoes

- 1 large Onion

- 4 large Eggs

- ⅓ cup Matzo Meal

- 1 Tablespoon Potato Starch

- 2 teaspoons Kosher Salt

- ½ teaspoon Freshly Ground Black Pepper

- ½ teaspoon Baking Powder optional

- Grapeseed Oil

DIRECTIONS:

1. Wash Potatoes and peel. Run through Food Processor to grate and then place in a Bowl with cool waters. Set aside.

2. Rinse out Food Processor and grate Onions. Place Onion in Tea Towel or Paper Towel and squeeze out all liquid.

3. In a medium mixing bowl, whisk together Eggs. Add Salt, Pepper, Matzo Meal, Potato Starch, Baking Powder (if using) and grated Onions.

4. Drain Water from Potatoes and save the Starch left in the Bowl. Squeeze out all water from Potatoes and add to Onion Mixture. Scoop out the Starch from the Potato Bowl and add to Latkes mixture.

5. Generously spray Silicone Trays with Oil. Fill each well with the Latkes Mixture and generously spray with Oil.

6. Air Fry at 350 degrees for 6 minutes. Remove Air Fryer Basket and pop out Bites into Air Fryer. Spray generously and cook for 4 additional minutes at 400 degrees. Serve with Applesauce and Sour Cream.

CINNAMON ROLLS

Serves: 4

Cook Time: 15 minutes

INGREDIENTS:

- 1 pound frozen bread dough, thawed
- ¼ cup butter, melted and cooled
- ¾ cup brown sugar
- 1½ tablespoons ground cinnamon
- Cream Cheese Glaze:
- 4 ounces cream cheese, softened
- 2 tablespoons butter, softened
- 1¼ cups powdered sugar
- ½ teaspoon vanilla

DIRECTIONS:

1. Let the bread dough come to room temperature on the counter. On a lightly floured surface roll the dough into a 13-inch by 11-inch rectangle. Position the rectangle so the 13-inch side is facing you. Brush the melted butter all over the dough, leaving a 1-inch border uncovered along the edge farthest away from you.

2. Combine the brown sugar and cinnamon in a small bowl. Sprinkle the mixture evenly over the buttered dough, keeping the 1-inch border

uncovered. Roll the dough into a log starting with the edge closest to you. Roll the dough tightly, making sure to roll evenly and push out any air pockets. When you get to the uncovered edge of the dough, press the dough onto the roll to seal it together.

3. Cut the log into 8 pieces, slicing slowly with a sawing motion so you don't flatten the dough. Turn the slices on their sides and cover with a clean kitchen towel. Let the rolls sit in the warmest part of your kitchen for 1½ to 2 hours to rise.

4. To make the glaze, place the cream cheese and butter in a microwave-safe bowl. Soften the mixture in the microwave for 30 seconds at a time until it is easy to stir. Gradually add the powdered sugar and stir to combine. Add the vanilla extract and whisk until smooth. Set aside.

5. When the rolls have risen, pre-heat the air fryer to 350°F.

6. Transfer 4 of the rolls to the air fryer basket. Air-fry for 5 minutes. Turn the rolls over and air-fry for another 4 minutes. Repeat with the remaining 4 rolls.

7. Let the rolls cool for a couple of minutes before glazing. Spread large dollops of cream cheese glaze on top of the warm cinnamon rolls, allowing some of the glaze to drip down the side of the rolls. Serve warm and enjoy!

HOT CHICKEN

Serves: 4

Cook Time: 20 minutes

INGREDIENTS:

- 1 (4-pound) chicken, cut into 6 pieces (2 breasts, 2 thighs and 2 drumsticks)

- 2 eggs

- 1 cup buttermilk

- 2 cups all-purpose flour

- 2 tablespoons paprika

- 1 teaspoon garlic powder

- 1 teaspoon onion powder

- 2 teaspoons salt

- 1 teaspoon freshly ground black pepper

- vegetable oil

- Nashville Hot Sauce:

- 1 tablespoon cayenne pepper

- 1 teaspoon salt

- ¼ cup vegetable oil

- 4 slices white bread

- dill pickle slices

DIRECTIONS:

1. Cut the chicken breasts into 2 pieces so that you have a total of 8 pieces of chicken.

2. Set up a two-stage dredging station. Whisk the eggs and buttermilk together in a bowl. Combine the flour, paprika, garlic powder, onion powder, salt and black pepper in a zipper-sealable plastic bag. Dip the chicken pieces into the egg-buttermilk mixture, then toss them in the seasoned flour, coating all sides. Repeat this procedure (egg mixture and then flour mixture) one more time. This can be a little messy, but make sure all sides of the chicken are completely covered. Spray the chicken with vegetable oil and set aside.

3. Pre-heat the air fryer to 370°F. Spray or brush the bottom of the air-fryer basket with a little vegetable oil.

4. Air-fry the chicken in two batches at 370°F for 20 minutes, flipping the pieces over halfway through the cooking process. Transfer the chicken to a plate, but do not cover. Repeat with the second batch of chicken.

5. Lower the temperature on the air fryer to 340°F. Flip the chicken back over and place the first batch of chicken on top of the second batch already in the basket. Air-fry for another 7 minutes.

6. While the chicken is air-frying, combine the cayenne pepper and salt in a bowl. Heat the vegetable oil in a small saucepan and when it is very hot, add it to the spice mix, whisking until smooth. It will sizzle briefly when you add it to the spices. Place the fried chicken on top of the white bread slices and brush the hot sauce all over chicken. Top with the pickle slices and serve warm. Enjoy the heat and the flavor!

BAKED RICOTTA WITH LEMON AND CAPERS

Serves: 4

Cook Time: 20 minutes

INGREDIENTS:

- 7-inch pie dish or cake pan
- 1½ cups whole milk ricotta cheese
- zest of 1 lemon, plus more for garnish
- 1 teaspoon finely chopped fresh rosemary
- pinch crushed red pepper flakes
- 2 tablespoons capers, rinsed
- 2 tablespoons extra-virgin olive oil
- salt and freshly ground black pepper
- 1 tablespoon grated Parmesan cheese

DIRECTIONS:

1. Pre-heat the air fryer to 380°F.

2. Combine the ricotta cheese, lemon zest, rosemary, red pepper flakes, capers, olive oil, salt and pepper in a bowl and whisk together well. Transfer to a 7-inch pie dish and place in the air fryer basket. You can use an aluminum foil sling to help with this by taking a long piece of

aluminum foil, folding it in half lengthwise twice until it looks like it is about 26-inches by 3-inches.

3. Place this under the pie dish and hold the ends of the foil to move the pie dish in and out of the air fryer basket. Tuck the ends of the foil beside the pie dish while it cooks in the air fryer.

4. Air-fry at 380°F for 8 to 10 minutes, or until the top is nicely browned in spots.

5. Remove from the air fryer and immediately sprinkle the Parmesan cheese on top. Drizzle a little more olive oil on top and add some freshly ground black pepper and some lemon zest as garnish. Serve warm with pita chips or crostini.

AIR-FRIED BEIGNETS

Serves: 4

Cook Time: 20 minutes

INGREDIENTS:

- ¾ cup lukewarm water (about 90°F)

- ¼ cup sugar

- 1 generous teaspoon active dry yeast (½ envelope)

- 3½ to 4 cups all-purpose flour

- ½ teaspoon salt

- 2 tablespoons unsalted butter, room temperature and cut into small pieces

- 1 egg, lightly beaten

- ½ cup evaporated milk

- ¼ cup melted butter

- 1 cup confectioners' sugar

- chocolate sauce or raspberry sauce, to dip

DIRECTIONS:

1. Combine the lukewarm water, a pinch of the sugar and the yeast in a
    bowl and let it proof for 5 minutes. It should froth a little. If it doesn't
    froth, your yeast is not active and you should start again with new yeast.

2. Combine 3½ cups of the flour, salt, 2 tablespoons of butter and the
    remaining sugar in a large bowl, or in the bowl of a stand mixer. Add
    the egg, evaporated milk and yeast mixture to the bowl and mix with
    a wooden spoon (or the paddle attachment of the stand mixer) until
    the dough comes together in a sticky ball. Add a little more flour if
    necessary to get the dough to form. Transfer the dough to an oiled
    bowl, cover with plastic wrap or a clean kitchen towel and let it rise in a
    warm place for at least 2 hours or until it has doubled in bulk. Longer is
    better for flavor development and you can even let the dough rest in the
    refrigerator overnight (just remember to bring it to room temperature
    before proceeding with the recipe).

3. Roll the dough out to ½-inch thickness. Cut the dough into rectangular
    or diamond-shaped pieces. You can make the beignets any size you like,
    but this recipe will give you 24 (2-inch x 3-inch) rectangles.

4. Pre-heat the air fryer to 350°F.

5. Brush the beignets on both sides with some of the melted butter and
    air-fry in batches at 350°F for 5 minutes, turning them over halfway
    through if desired. (They will brown on all sides without being flipped,
    but flipping them will brown them more evenly.)

6. As soon as the beignets are finished, transfer them to a plate or baking
    sheet and dust with the confectioners' sugar. Serve warm with a
    chocolate or raspberry sauce.

4. VEGAN DINNERS

TOFU BUDDHA BOWL

Serves: 4

Cook Time: 20 minutes

INGREDIENTS:

- 1 14ounce package extra firm tofu
- 2 Tbsp. sesame oil
- 1/4 cup soy sauce
- 3 Tbsp. molasses (or maple syrup)
- 2 Tbsp. lime juice
- 1 Tbsp. Sriracha
- 1 lb. fresh romanesco (or broccoli) - florets only
- 3 medium carrots - peeled, thinly sliced
- 1 red bell pepper - thinly sliced
- 8 oz. fresh spinach - sautéed with garlic and olive oil
- 2 cups cooked red quinoa

DIRECTIONS:

1. Wrap tofu in a several paper towels and set a plate on top to press out excess liquid. Once dry, unwrap tofu and cut into very small cubes (about 100 pieces).

2. Add sesame oil, soy sauce, molasses, lime juice, and Sriracha to a large bowl and whisk until incorporated.

3. Add tofu to the sauce and let marinate for 5-10 minutes, stirring occasionally.

4. Preheat air fryer to 370 degrees for 3 minutes.

5. Remove tofu from bowl and add to air fryer basket, leaving all marinade in bowl. Cook tofu for 15 minutes, shaking basket every 5 minutes.

6. Meanwhile, add romanesco, carrots, and bell pepper to bowl with marinade and mix well every few minutes.

7. Once tofu is done, remove from air fryer and set aside. Then add vegetables to air fryer basket, again leaving marinade in bowl. Cook vegetables for 10 minutes, giving the basket a good shake halfway through cook time.

8. In a large serving bowl - begin to build your Buddha Bowl. First add cooked quinoa, then spread the cooked veggies evenly. Next add the cooked spinach, and finally the tofu. Pour over remaining marinade and garnish with sesame seeds.

9. Bring to the table for everyone to dig in. Enjoy!

AIR-FRIED
FALAFEL

Serves: 4

Cook Time: 20 minutes

INGREDIENTS:

- Crispy Falafel
- 2 cups dried chickpeas
- 1 onion, diced
- 2 cloves garlic, minced
- ¾ cup flat-leaf parsley leaves
- ¼ cup cilantro leaves
- 1 Tbsp. chickpea flour
- 2 tsp. ground cumin
- 2 tsp. ground coriander
- 1 tsp. ground black pepper
- ½ tsp. cayenne pepper
- 1 ½ tsp. sea salt
- Tahini Sauce
- ¼ cup tahini
- 2 tsp. maple syrup
- ½ lemon, juiced
- 2-4 Tbsp. water, to thin
- sea salt, to taste

DIRECTIONS:

1. Falafel

2. Place dry (unsoaked, uncooked) chickpeas into a big bowl, cover them with cold water, and let them soak for 24 hours. Once soaked, drain and rinse the chickpeas.

3. Place all the Ingredients into a food processor and pulse until the chickpeas are finely minced. Do not over-pulse the mixture should be coarse, not smooth/paste-y,

4. Using your hands, shape the falafel mixture into small balls (about 1.5" in diameter). Arrange about 9 falafel balls in a single layer in your air fryer basket and air-fry for about 15 minutes at 380° F. The falafel is done when it's golden brown and crisp. Store the falafel in a warm place until ready to serve.

5. Tahini Sauce

6. Mix the tahini, maple syrup, lemon juice, and salt in a small bowl. Add 1 Tbsp. of water at a time to reach the desired consistency.

AIR-FRIED BUFFALO CAULIFLOWER STEAKS

Serves: 4

Cook Time: 20 minutes

INGREDIENTS:

- for the cauliflower
- one large head of cauliflower
- salt and pepper
- for the dry Ingredients
- 1 ½ cups AP flour
- ⅓ cup cornstarch
- 1 TB garlic powder
- 1 TB onion powder
- 1 TB salt
- 1 TB paprika
- 2 tsp cayenne (optional)
- for the wet Ingredients
- 1 cup soymilk, with 2 tsp apple cider vinegar whisked in
- 2 TB Follow Your Heart VeganEgg powder, blended with ½ cup ice cold water
- 2 TB bourbon

- 1 TB hot sauce

- for frying and coating

- Spray oil

- at least one cup of prepared buffalo sauce. (You can also make your own by mixing a 1:1 ratio of melted vegan butter with a vinegar-based hot sauce)

- to serve

- toasted hamburger buns

- cabbage or lettuce

- pickles

- red onion

- tomato and/or avocado

- vegan bleu cheese dressing

- extra buffalo sauce

- celery

DIRECTIONS:

1. To prep the cauliflower

2. To cut your cauliflower steaks, place a head of cauliflower stem side down on a cutting board. Using a large knife, slice it down the very middle. Then cut down again on each half to create 3 or 4, 1-inch thick slabs. Chop up the leftover portion of the cauliflower into little, bite-sized florets.

3. Bring a large pot of salted water to a boil. Place the cauliflower into the pot, let the boil return, wait about a minute, then transfer the florets to a cookie sheet with a wire rack over it to cool. Sprinkle with salt and

pepper. Leave out for 30 minutes, or throw into your refrigerator to cool.

4. to make the breading

5. Combine all of the dry Ingredients together in a medium-sized bowl.

6. Combine all of the wet Ingredients into a separate medium-sized bowl.

7. Working one piece at a time, coat the steaks and florets evenly in the dry mixture, tapping off any extra and placing it back onto the wire rack.

8. Pour 3 tablespoons of the wet mixture into the dry mixture and combine with a rubber spatula.

9. Working one piece at a time, dunk the steaks and florets into the wet mixture, then pack the moistened flour mixture firmly around it.

10. Return the battered cauliflower back onto the wire rack and place into the refrigerator to chill for at least 30 minutes.

11. to air fry the cauliflower

12. Spray the cauliflower steaks evenly with cooking spray. Place into the air fryer at 400 degrees and cook for 10 minutes, flipping the slabs over halfway through the cooking time. Apply a little more spray over any areas that look dry and cook for an additional minute or two if needed to achieve a deeply golden color all over.

13. Place the buffalo sauce into a bowl, then carefully turn the steaks around in the bowl to coat. Place back into the air fryer and fry on each side for 3-4 minutes, or until the edges look crispy.

14. Repeat the process with the florets. Air fry time will take less with the florets since they are smaller. Just give them a shake halfway through the cook time, and spray any areas with cooking spray that look dry.

15. Serve immediately on toasted hamburger buns or with celery and vegan bleu cheese dressing.

AIR FRYER SOURDOUGH BOULE

Serves: 4

Cook Time: 25 minutes

INGREDIENTS:

- 1 cup sourdough starter
- 1 cup unbleached all-purpose flour
- ¼ cup 100% whole wheat flour
- 1 tablespoon sugar
- ½ teaspoon sea salt
- 1 tablespoon olive oil

DIRECTIONS:

1. Combine Ingredients, in the order listed in a bread machine. Choose the dough only setting (typically 1 hour

2. and 28 minutes) to mix, knead and rise (be sure that the «heat» function is off - you do not want to bake in

3. the machine!). If you're not using a bread machine, use whatever method you prefer for the mixing and

4. kneading process.

5. Once the dough function is complete, remove the paddles from the bread machine and allow the dough to

6. Rise/ferment for four hours.

7. After four hours, transfer the dough to a floured proofing basket to rise for three more hours.

8. Just before you»re ready to air fry, preheat the air fryer for 3 minutes at 390°F. Gently flip the dough over, out of proofing basket, onto the grill insert in the air fryer (you want the bottom of the dough, with the proofing basket rings, on top.

9. Air fry for 20 minutes at 390°F, gently shaking at 10 minutes. Before removing from the air fryer, check the

10. internal temperature with a kitchen thermometer to ensure the bread is between 190 to 200°F.

11. Transfer the boule to a baking rack. Allow the loaf to cool for 2 to 3 hours before slicing.

CAULIFLOWER CHICKEN

Serves: 4

Cook Time: 20 minutes

INGREDIENTS:

- 1 cup all purpose flour
- 1 tablespoon arrowroot powder or cornstarch
- ½ teaspoon salt
- ½ teaspoon cayenne pepper
- ½ teaspoon white pepper
- ½ teaspoon onion powder
- ½ teaspoon garlic powder
- ½ teaspoon sweet or smoked paprika
- ¼ teaspoon Old Bay seasoning
- 1 tablespoon nutritional yeast
- ⅓ cup hot sauce
- ¼ cup unsweetened plain soy milk or other non-dairy milk
- 1 tablespoon Dijon mustard
- 5 cups safflower oil, or other frying oil
- 1 large head of cauliflower, cut into large florets

DIRECTIONS:

1. In a medium-sized mixing bowl combine the flour, arrowroot powder, salt, cayenne pepper, white pepper, onion powder, garlic powder, paprika, Old Bay, and nutritional yeast.

2. In another bowl combine the hot sauce, soy milk, and Dijon mustard and whisk until creamy.

3. Heat the frying oil in a large dutch oven or fryer. It should be around 350°.

4. Use one hand to carefully dip a cauliflower floret into the wet mixture, then drop it into the flour mixture. Use your other hand (it should be dry) to coat it completely. Dip it back into the hot sauce mixture, and again into the dry mixture, keeping one hand devoted to wet and one to dry.

5. Carefully lower the twice coated cauliflower into the hot oil. Repeat with remaining cauliflower until you can't fit any more into the pot. Cook for about 4-5 minutes, until the pieces are golden.

6. Transfer fried cauliflower to a large plate covered with two sheets of paper towel to absorb excess oil.

7. Continue to cook the remaining cauliflower.

8. Serve hot.

VEGAN
FRIED RAVIOLI

Serves: 4

Cook Time: 10 minutes

INGREDIENTS:

- ½ cup panko bread crumbs
- 2 teaspoons nutritional yeast flakes
- 1 teaspoon dried basil
- 1 teaspoon dried oregano
- 1 teaspoon garlic powder
- Pinch of salt & pepper
- ¼ cup aquafaba (liquid from can of chickpeas or other beans)
- 8 ounces frozen or thawed vegan ravioli
- Spritz of cooking spray
- ½ cup marinara (for dipping)

DIRECTIONS:

1. On a plate, combine panko bread crumbs, nutritional yeast flakes, dried basil, dried oregano, garlic powder, salt, and pepper.
2. Put aquafaba into a small separate bowl.

3. Dip ravioli into aquafaba, shake off excess liquid, and then dredge in bread crumb mixture. Make sure that the ravioli gets fully covered. Move the ravioli into the air fryer basket. Continue until all of the ravioli has been breaded. Be careful not to overlap the ravioli too much in the air fryer, so that they can brown evenly. (If necessary, air fry in batches.)

4. Spritz the ravioli with cooking spray.

5. Set air fryer to 390 degrees. Air fry for 6 minutes. Carefully flip each ravioli over. (Don›t just shake the basket. If you do, you›ll lose a lot of bread crumbs.) Air fry for 2 more minutes.

6. Remove ravioli from air fryer and serve with warm marinara for dipping.

VEGAN AIR FRIED CHICKEN

Serves: 4

Cook Time: 30 minutes

INGREDIENTS:

- Wet Batter/Marinade
- 2 medium sized mixing bowls
- 4 cups almond milk
- 1 Large Cauliflower
- 4 tbsp poultry seasoning
- 2 tsp seasoned salt
- Dry Batter
- 2 cups flour
- 1 cup bread crumbs (Panko if possible, I used Trader Joe's)
- 1 tbsp arrowroot powder
- 1 tbsp seasoned salt
- Creole Seasoning Mix
- 1 tsp paprika
- 1.5 tbsp garlic powder
- ¼ tsp pepper

- 1 tsp onion powder

- ½ tsp cayenne

- 1 tsp oregano

- 1 tsp thyme

- 1 tsp garlic salt

DIRECTIONS:

1. Wash and cut cauliflower into medium/large sized pieces. Combine wet batter/marinade Ingredients into two separate medium-sized mixing bowls. 2 cups almond milk, 2 tbsp poultry seasoning, and 1 tsp seasoned salt in each bowl. Mix Ingredients well, saturate cauliflower, and then refrigerate for a minimum of 4 hours or overnight.

2. Combine dry batter Ingredients. Add in Creole Seasoning mix. Mix well.

3. Grease the entire inside of the air fryer basket and rack (if applicable) with coconut oil.

4. Take one bowl of the marinated cauliflower out of the fridge and removed cauliflower from bowl. Using tongs, take each piece of cauliflower submerge in marinade mix. Shake off excess liquid and then toss in the dry batter mix. Once cauliflower is completely covered, shake off the excess and then dip back into the liquid. Dip the cauliflower in the dry batter again and then once more into the wet batter. Place cauliflower in greased air fryer basket. Repeat for all pieces and the second bowl of cauliflower.

5. Do not overfill the air fryer. Do not stack caulifower on top of each other. This might cause the pieces to stick together, not sure. I placed about 4 pieces into the basket at a time.

6. Cook at 392 degrees Fahrenheit for 25 minutes. After 10 minutes turn cauliflower.

7. After cooking all the pieces, you can toss them (stacked) back into the air fryer for 5 minutes if you need to reheat them or if they've been sitting out and you need to make them crispier. No need to turn them once cooked. They will keep in the fridge for 1-2 days.

8. Serve with honey mustard.

NACHO VEGAN MEATLOAF

Serves: 4

Cook Time: 25 minutes

INGREDIENTS:

- 8 ounces Beyond Meat 2 patties
- ¼ cup diced chopped yellow onion
- ¼ cup finely chopped carrot
- ½ cup chunky salsa jarred or homemade
- ½ teaspoon chili powder
- ¼ teaspoon sea salt
- ¼ teaspoon black pepper
- ¾ cup crumbled Beanfields Jalapeño Nacho Bean and Rice Chips
- 1 tablespoon VeganEgg powder
- ¼ cup cold water
- 2 tablespoons additional salsa
- ¼ cup shredded vegan cheddar cheese

DIRECTIONS:

1. Place Beyond Burger, onion, carrot, salsa, chili powder, salt, pepper, and crumbled chips in a large bowl. Set aside.

2. Add VeganEgg and cold water to a blender. Quickly pulse to blend. Pour into the large bowl.

3. Preheat the air fryer on 360°F for 3 minutes.

4. Back to the bowl, use your hands to combine the meaty mixture. Divide into two parts. Transfer one half to a5.7 x 3 x 2.1-inch mini loaf pan and transfer the other half to a second mini loaf pan.

5. Place the mini loaf pans in the air fryer basket and cook on 360°F for 20 minutes.

6. Remove the loaf pans from the air fryer and spread 1 tablespoon of salsa over the top of one loaf. Spread 1 tablespoon of salsa on the second loaf. Sprinkle ¼ cup shredded vegan cheddar cheese over one load and the other ¼ cup shredded vegan cheddar cheese over the second loaf. Return the loaf pans to the air fryer basket.

7. Increase the heat to 390°F and cook for 3 minutes longer.

BEAN AND GRAIN SOURDOUGH SLIDERS

Serves: 4

Cook Time: 15 minutes

INGREDIENTS:

- 1 ½ cups cooked scarlet runner beans
- ½ to ¾ cup mix of cooked brown basmati rice/farro
- ½ cup of diced onion
- ⅓ cup panko
- 4 cloves garlic
- Juice of half a lime
- 1 teaspoon salt
- ½ teaspoon cumin
- 1/ teaspoon Mexican oregano
- 1 teaspoons chipotle avocado oil
- 2 to 3 spritzes olive oil spray

DIRECTIONS:

1. Add the beans, grains, onion, panko, garlic, lime juice, salt, cumin, oregano, and avocado oil to a food processor. Pulse until roughly chopped and easy to form into patties.

2. Form 8 sliders - about ¼ cup mixture per slider. Refrigerate for two hours (or for several days).

3. Spritz the air fryer basket and the top of the sliders with olive oil.

4. Place in the air fryer and cook on 330°F for 10 minutes. Gently flip over, spritz tops again, and increase the

5. heat to 390°F to cook for 3 minutes longer.

CHEESY
POTATO WEDGES

Serves: 4

Cook Time: 20 minutes

INGREDIENTS::

- Potatoes
- 1 pound fingerling potatoes
- 1 teaspoon extra-virgin olive oil
- 1 teaspoon kosher salt
- 1 teaspoon ground black pepper
- ½ teaspoon garlic powder
- Cheese Sauce
- ½ cup raw cashews
- ½ teaspoon ground turmeric
- ½ teaspoon paprika
- 2 tablespoons nutritional yeast
- 1 teaspoon fresh lemon juice
- 2 tablespoons to ¼ cup water

DIRECTIONS:

1. Potatoes: Preheat the air fryer to 400°F for 3 minutes. Wash the potatoes. Cut the potatoes in half lengthwise and transfer them to a large bowl. Add the oil, salt, pepper, and garlic powder to the potatoes. Toss to coat. Transfer the potatoes to the air fryer. Cook for 16 minutes, shaking halfway through the cooking time.

2. Cheese Sauce: Combine the cashews, turmeric, paprika, nutritional yeast, and lemon juice in a high-speed blender. Blend on low, slowly increasing the speed and adding water as needed. Be careful to avoid using too much water, as you want a thick, cheesy consistency.

3. Transfer the cooked potatoes to an air fryer–safe pan or a piece of parchment paper. Drizzle the cheese sauce over the potato wedges. Place the pan in the air fryer and cook for 2 more minutes at 400°F.

Printed in the USA
CPSIA information can be obtained
at www.ICGtesting.com
LVHW052347021224
798169LV00009BA/276